Alpine Cocktails

Alpine Cocktails

POURS, DRINKS, SIPS, AND BITES

edited by ALLYSON REEDY
photographs by Greg McBoat

Gibbs Smith

First Edition
30 29 28 27 26 5 4 3 2 1

Published by
Gibbs Smith
Layton, Utah
www.gibbs-smith.com
The authorized representative in the EEA is Simon and Schuster Netherlands BV, Herculesplein 96 3584 AA Utrecht, Netherlands, info@simonandschuster.nl

Designed by Sheryl Dickert
Production design by Renee Bond

Library of Congress Control Number: 2026930009
ISBN: 978-1-4236-6964-7
Ebook ISBN: 978-1-4236-6965-4

Printed and bound in China using FSC®-certified and other controlled materials.

FSC www.fsc.org
MIX
Paper | Supporting responsible forestry
FSC® C144853

Contents

Introduction

Fact: You don't need to be a snow bunny or powder hound to appreciate après-ski culture. From the French term meaning "after ski," this isn't just a catchphrase or time of day. Après-ski is a state of mind. A cozy, hygge-loaded, wintry state of mind.

Alpine style doesn't care whether you're carving double black diamonds at sunrise or if you just like wearing cute sweaters. That's because alpine style is more than just chairlifts and powder days. It's the camaraderie and coziness of snuggling by a crackling fire, well-made drink in hand.

Whether it's an espresso martini in Telluride, a cherry-ginger spritz in the Swiss Alps, or a spiked hot chocolate on your couch in Louisiana, you can channel mountain vibes anywhere. Because no matter your locale's weather or altitude, après-ski is for you.

In this book, you'll find recipes for the cocktails, mocktails, spritzes, and hot sippers that will transport you to snowy peaks and toasty lodges. The drinks are created by iconic bars and resorts around the world, from the Rockies to the Alps, all dreamed up and perfected by master mixologists who live and breathe après-ski culture.

The point of après-ski is to wind down and get comfortable, so lean in to the relaxation and don't stress too much about these recipes. Some mixologists have recommended their favorite spirit brands, but feel free to use whatever brand of bourbon, gin, brandy, fill-in-the-blank spirit you have at home. While you may want to glance over the recipes and pick up some new ingredients for your bar cart the next time you're at the grocery or liquor store, so long as you have a healthy roster of brown spirits, bitter aperitifs, a bottle of bubbles, and a little citrus, you're most of the way there.

Other ditch-the-stress, embrace-the-alpine lifestyle tips: Garnishes are pretty much always optional, and glassware is a suggestion. Your drink will look and feel next-level gussied up with a cinnamon stick and freshly grated nutmeg on top, but guess what? It'll taste just as good without it. Aesthetics are important, yes, but don't let your lack of at-the-ready garnishes stop you from enjoying a great drink. Stress isn't cozy.

WHO THE RECIPES COME FROM

These drinks are gifted to us from leading mixologists and bartenders who spend their days and nights fulfilling the cocktail dreams of ski bunnies around the world. They shake, stir, and hot toddy it up for a living, coming from bars, restaurants, and resorts with serious altitude. Nobody knows après-ski like these folks.

Sometimes these pros note a specific brand they like to use in their recipes, but don't feel constrained to only those bottles. If an ingredient or spirit might be hard to find, I've listed a close substitute, and when exact liquid measurements are left off (such as soda water or bubbly for topping), it's because it depends on the glass you're using or your desired concentration.

WHERE TO SOURCE INGREDIENTS

Most of what you need to whip up a killer spritz or cold-weather cocktail can be found at your local grocery and liquor store. But a few recipes might require a bit more looking to do them justice. (Specialty stores and online retailers can be great resources.)

Some recipes require infused spirits or syrups. This may sound difficult, but it's actually as easy as pouring and waiting. For example, the Chamomile Tea Infused Brandy for the Short Skirt and Long Jacket on page 66: The only effort you have to put in is dumping the tea into the brandy. It's the same with simple syrup, where you're boiling sugar, water, and whatever ingredient is going to punch up your drink.

SIMPLE SYRUP

Here's a basic simple syrup recipe, but to jazz it up with flavors like lavender or rosemary, all you do is add the bonus ingredient to the pan.

MAKES 1½ CUPS; 1:1 SUGAR TO WATER RATIO

1 cup water
1 cup sugar

Combine the sugar and the water in a medium saucepan over medium heat. Bring to a boil and stir until the sugar fully dissolves. Remove from the heat and allow to cool for 15 minutes. Pour into a sterilized jar, add the lid, label, and store for up to 1 month in the refrigerator.

BLUEBERRY SYRUP: Stir in 1 cup blueberries with the water and sugar. Boil, strain, and store as directed.

CINNAMON SYRUP: Stir in 1 cinnamon stick with the water and sugar. Boil, strain, and store as directed.

DEMERARA SYRUP: Swap demerara sugar for white sugar. Boil, strain, and store as directed.

GINGER SYRUP: Stir in ½ cup peeled, chopped ginger with the water and sugar. Boil, strain, and store as directed.

HONEY SYRUP: Swap honey for white sugar. Boil, strain, and store as directed.

LAVENDER SYRUP: Stir in ¼ cup lavender with the water and sugar. Boil, strain, and store as directed.

MINT AND CINNAMON SYRUP: Stir in ½ cup fresh mint leaves and 2 to 3 cinnamon sticks with the water and sugar. Boil, strain, and store as directed.

PINK PEPPERCORN SYRUP: Add 3 tablespoons pink peppercorns with the water and sugar. Boil, strain, and store as directed.

ROSEMARY SYRUP: Add ¼ cup fresh rosemary leaves with the water and sugar. Boil, strain, and store as directed.

TURBINADO SYRUP: Swap turbinado sugar for white sugar. Boil, strain, and store as directed.

VIOLET SYRUP: Add 1 cup organic violet flowers (green parts removed) with the water and sugar. Boil, strain, and store as directed.

SALINE SOLUTION

A few recipes call for saline solution, which is as easy as stirring salt into water.

MAKES ⅓ CUP; 1:4 SALT TO WATER RATIO

⅓ cup hot water
1 tablespoon (20 grams) kosher salt

Pour the water and salt into a jar and stir until salt is dissolved. Allow it to sit for a few minutes until the mixture is clear. Pour mixture into a dropper bottle and store in a cool, dark place.

EQUIPMENT YOU'LL NEED

Besides the liquid ingredients, there are just a few more things you need to get going on your alpine cocktail adventure. While heavy packers can also load up their bar carts with fancy ice molds, peelers, and siphons, this list is for those who prefer to travel light.

Citrus Juicer

Fresh tastes better than bottled. It just does. A handheld juicer is perfect for making fresh-squeezed lemon and lime juice.

Fine-Mesh Strainer

This is used for straining ice and other solids out of drinks before you pour them into the glass. It's also helpful when making simple syrups and spirit infusions.

Glasses

You need something to hold that delicious cocktail you just shook up. Practically speaking, any glass will do, but it's scientifically proven that drinks taste better when sipped out of cool cups. The cocktails and mocktails in this book utilize all sorts of glasses, including mugs, rocks, collins, coupes, martinis, and goblets.

Ice

The unsung hero of cocktails and mocktails! Used for blending, shaking, mixing, and cooling, ice is critical. You can get by with standard-sized cubes, you can use crushed or pebble, or you can kick it up a notch with giant cubes and spheres. Remember, the smaller the cube, the faster it melts, thus diluting the drink.

Jigger/Measuring Glass

A jigger is a two-sided measuring tool for pouring liquor. You can also use a shot glass or other measuring glass that denotes ounces.

Muddler

Some drinks require herbs or fruit to be smashed to get their essence into the drink. If you don't have a dedicated muddler, you can also use the back of a wooden spoon.

Shaker

There are different types of shaking devices out there, including the Boston (with a metal shaking tin and glass mixing tin), the Parisian (both shaking and mixing tins are metal), and the Cobbler (the one you likely have at home with a metal shaking tin, lid with built-in holes for straining, and a cap). So long as you've got one of these, you're good to go.

Stir Stick/Bar Spoon

Basically, any long-handled, narrow device that can stir up your drink works.

And finally, what are you waiting for? Après all day!

Cozy Cocktails

"I think I missed my calling as an après-ski instructor."

—ANONYMOUS

THE SUNBURNT SKIER

ELEVEN SCARP RIDGE LODGE, CRESTED BUTTE, CO

You won't get burned with this bright, unexpected drink, where the blend of tequila, Aperol, and elderflower hits like skis on fresh powder. It's après-ski meets elderflower's alpine bloom.

SERVES 1

1½ ounces tequila blanco
½ ounce Aperol, or other bitter orange liqueur
½ ounce elderflower liqueur
¾ ounce lemon juice
½ orange wheel, for garnish

GLASS: rocks

Add ice to the large side of a shaker. Pour tequila, Aperol, elderflower liqueur, and lemon juice into the small side of the shaker. Give it a good shake and strain into a rocks glass filled with a large ice cube. Garnish with orange.

ALPINE MULE

BÜRGENSTOCK RESORT LAKE LUCERNE, SWITZERLAND

A mule, but make it mountain. At Bürgenstock Resort Lake Lucerne, they use Appenzeller, a Swiss herbal liqueur, but you can swap another bitter aperitif if you have trouble finding it. Use a good quality ginger beer for extra bite.

SERVES 1

1 ounce Appenzeller, or other bitter aperitif
⅓ ounce Lillet Blanc
½ ounce lime juice
Ginger beer
Rosemary sprig, for garnish

GLASS: copper mug

Pour bitter aperitif, Lillet Blanc, and lime juice into tumbler and give it a stir. Add ice and top with ginger beer. Stir and garnish with rosemary.

WINTER'S HARVEST

MINUS5° ICEBAR, LAS VEGAS, NV

The best place to cool down in Vegas is at one of the Minus5° ICEBARs, where drinkers don parkas and gloves to chill out in the negative five degrees Celsius lounge. The Winter's Harvest cocktail—a mix of spiced rum, cranberry, lime, and ginger beer—is a bold, bubbly, Vegas-worthy holiday party starter.

SERVES 1

1½ ounces spiced rum
2 ounces cranberry juice
½ ounce lime juice
Ginger beer
Mint, for garnish
Lime wheel, for garnish

GLASS: rocks

Pour spiced rum, cranberry juice, and lime juice into a rocks glass. Give it a stir and fill glass with ice. Top with ginger beer and garnish with mint and lime.

BEAR PAW BRAMBLE

JOSEPH NEWTON, THE LOOKOUT BAR, AVON, CO

Almost too pretty to drink, this jewel-toned sipper is fruity, tart, and floral. The honey and jammy fruit from the blackberry liqueur sweeten up the gin and red verjus (which is like grape juice, if grape juice wore Chanel and spoke French) adds even more richness.

SERVES 1

1½ ounces gin
½ ounce blackberry liqueur
½ ounce red verjus
½ ounce honey
½ ounce lemon juice

GLASS: rocks

Pour gin, blackberry liqueur, red verjus, honey, and lemon juice into a shaker tin with ice. Give it a good shake and strain into a rocks glass filled with crushed ice.

THE DEATH STAR

HIDALGO AT W ASPEN IN COLLABORATION WITH DUSHAN ZARIĆ, ASPEN, CO

The espresso martini is a slopeside essential for its combo of caffeine (hello, energy boost!) and downright deliciousness. They kick it up a notch in Aspen with orange bitters and by swapping vodka for tequila. Enjoy the double buzz.

SERVES 1

2 ounces Charbay Espresso Cocktail, or other coffee liqueur
1 ounce Tapatio tequila reposado, or other tequila reposado
1½ ounces espresso
2 drops Saline Solution (page 10)
2 drops orange bitters
1 teaspoon hot chocolate powder
Grated nutmeg, for garnish
Orange peel, for garnish

GLASS: martini

Pour all ingredients, except for the garnishes, into a shaker filled with ice. Give it a good shake and strain into a martini glass. Garnish with nutmeg and orange.

BARREL-AGED OLD FASHIONED

MINUS5° ICEBAR, LAS VEGAS, NV

What's better than an old fashioned on a wintry day? An old fashioned with a hit of amaro and orange liqueur. Perfect for sipping by the fire, under a fuzzy blanket, or pretty much wherever you are right now.

SERVES 1

2½ ounces Wild Turkey 81 proof bourbon, or other high-proof bourbon
½ ounce Pierre Ferrand Dry Curaçao, or other orange liqueur
½ ounce Amaro Averna, or other amaro
2 dashes aromatic bitters
2 dashes orange bitters
Orange peel, for garnish

GLASS: double rocks

Add a large ice sphere to a double rocks glass. Pour bourbon, orange liqueur, amaro, and both bitters into a mixing glass filled with ice. Give it a good stir and strain into the prepared glass. Garnish with orange.

EGGNOG

HANNAH HOPKINS (ADAPTED FROM DAN BUBENHEIM), YAMPA VALLEY KITCHEN, STEAMBOAT SPRINGS, CO

Eggnog might be a holiday, wintry drink, but we say why limit it to a couple of months out of the year? This batch cocktail, which adds softened vanilla bean ice cream to the mix, can last in the fridge for months (yes, really) and tastes like a festive, frothy, almost-milkshake. It's definitely all it's cracked up to be.

SERVES 5 TO 6

6 eggs, separated
1¾ cups powdered sugar
1 cup heavy cream
1 cup softened (not melted) vanilla bean ice cream
1 (375-milliliter) bottle dark or spiced rum
Grated nutmeg, plus extra for garnish

GLASS: coupe or glass of choice

SPECIAL EQUIPMENT: electric or handheld mixer

In a large bowl, use an electric or handheld mixer to whip egg whites into stiff peaks. Set aside. In a separate bowl, whip egg yolks and powdered sugar until pale yellow. Gently fold into the egg whites.

In a separate bowl, whip heavy cream to soft peaks and fold into the egg white mixture. Next, fold in the softened ice cream. Stir in the rum and grate fresh nutmeg to taste. Pour into coupe glasses and garnish with more nutmeg.

To store, refrigerate in a sealed container and it will last for months.

MATCHA MINT GARDEN & TONIC

RENA DAY, YAMPA VALLEY KITCHEN, STEAMBOAT SPRINGS, CO

Definitely channeling a wild mint patch in the mountains, you can almost count this cocktail as healthy. Between the ounce of green juice loaded with vitamins and the matcha powder with its antioxidants, you're practically cleansing here. (Don't worry, the simple syrup and gin make it delicious.)

SERVES 1

1½ ounces gin
1½ ounces Mint Syrup (below)
1 ounce lime juice
1 ounce green juice
1 tablespoon unsweetened matcha powder
Tonic water
Cucumber slice, for garnish
Mint sprig, for garnish

GLASS: goblet

Add gin, mint simple syrup, lime and green juices, and matcha powder to a shaker filled with ice. Shake well for a couple of seconds and strain into a goblet glass filled with ice. Top with tonic water and garnish with cucumber and mint.

Mint Syrup

MAKES 1 CUP

½ cup turbinado sugar
½ cup boiling water
½ cup fresh mint leaves

Pour all ingredients into a heatproof bowl. Stir well until sugar dissolves. Let sit for at least 30 minutes, or up to 12 hours. Strain into a Mason jar or other airtight container and store in the refrigerator for up to 2 weeks.

TIPSY CARROT

HANNAH HOPKINS, BÉSAME, STEAMBOAT SPRINGS, CO

How do you make a margarita mountain style? You bring an earthy kick to it, that's how. In Steamboat Springs, they add fresh carrot juice and chile simple syrup to the traditional tequila and lime, creating a drink that's not just eye-catching (but seriously, just look at that orange!) but also super bright and unique.

SERVES 1

1½ ounces Suerte blanco tequila, or other blanco tequila
1½ ounces carrot juice
1 ounce lime juice
¾ ounce Chile Syrup (below)
4 dashes habanero bitters
Smoked salt, for rim
Fresno chile, for garnish
Cilantro sprig, for garnish

GLASS: margarita

Add tequila, carrot juice, lime juice, chile syrup, and habanero bitters to a shaker filled with ice. Shake well for a couple of seconds. Strain the mixture into a margarita glass rimmed with salt. Garnish with Fresno chile and cilantro.

Chile Syrup

MAKES ABOUT 2 CUPS

½ jalapeño
½ Fresno chile
1 cup sugar
1 cup boiling water

Place both pepper halves in heatproof bowl. To heatproof bowl, add sugar and top with boiling water. Stir to dissolve sugar and let cool for 30 minutes, up to 12 hours. Strain into a Mason jar or other airtight container and store in the refrigerator for up to 2 weeks.

WINTER SANGRIA

LIBERTY ADAMS, BÉSAME, STEAMBOAT SPRINGS, CO

Sangria isn't just for summer sipping. This winter version—bursting with cozy cinnamon, apple, and brandy flavors—is perfect for even the coldest days. Even better? It tastes more fantastic the next day, after the fruit and wine have melded together.

SERVES 5

1 (750-milliliter) bottle red wine
¼ cup brandy
1 orange, cut into wedges
½ lemon, cut into wedges
½ apple, sliced
1 cinnamon stick
1½ teaspoons sugar

GLASS: pitcher or glass of choice

Mix all ingredients together in a large pitcher and steep in the fridge for up to 2 days.

PALOMA BRAVA

HIDALGO AT W ASPEN IN COLLABORATION WITH DUSHAN ZARIĆ, ASPEN, CO

Like a Mexican fiesta in the Rockies, this take on the paloma is just as good slopeside as it is poolside. Bright, fizzy, and balanced, the Tajin rim warms you up with its salty, sour heat.

SERVES 1

Tajin, for rim
2 ounces blanco tequila
1 ounce grapefruit cordial
½ ounce lime juice
2 drops Saline Solution (page 10)
2 dashes Miracle Mile celery bitters, or other celery bitters
3 ounces Fever Tree grapefruit soda, or other grapefruit soda
Dehydrated lime wheel, for garnish

GLASS: collins or glass of choice

Wet the rim of the collins glass and dip or roll the rim into the Tajin. Shake off the excess and add a few ice cubes to the glass. Add tequila, grapefruit cordial, lime juice, saline solution, and celery bitters into a shaker filled with ice. Give it a good shake and strain into the prepared glass. Top with grapefruit soda and garnish with dehydrated lime.

YELLOW JACKET

HIDALGO AT W ASPEN IN COLLABORATION WITH DUSHAN ZARIĆ, ASPEN, CO

Hidalgo, by Dushan Zarić (co-founder of Employees Only, which basically lives on every "world's best bars" list), is an agave temple. Of course this bittersweet cocktail celebrates mezcal in the best possible way: with elderflower liqueur, Yellow Chartreuse, and lots of bitters, because that's the way mezcal rolls.

SERVES 1

2 ounces Peloton de la Muerte Espadin mezcal, or other mezcal
½ ounce St-Germain, or other elderflower liqueur
½ ounce Lustau Manzanilla Papirusa sherry, or other Manzanilla sherry
¼ ounce Yellow Chartreuse
4 dashes Regan's Orange Bitters No. 6, or other orange bitters
4 dashes Angostura bitters
Lemon twist, for garnish

GLASS: coupe or glass of choice

Pour all ingredients, except for garnish, into a shaker filled with ice. Give it a good shake and strain into a coupe glass. Garnish with lemon.

SARONNO SOUR

SAVERINA, KIMPTON CLARET, DENVER, CO

Named for the northern Italian town that created amaretto—the sweet, almond-flavored liqueur—in the sixteenth century, the Saronno Sour is rounded out with cognac and lemon and shaken with an egg white to give it a rich, frothy mouthfeel.

SERVES 1

1½ ounces Grove Street amaretto, or other amaretto
½ ounce Hennessy, or other cognac
¾ ounce lemon juice
1 egg white
Angostura bitters, for garnish

GLASS: coupe

Add all ingredients, except the garnish, to a shaker without ice. Shake vigorously to add air and fluff the egg white. Add ice and shake 10 to 15 seconds more to chill the mixture. Pour through a fine-mesh strainer into a coupe glass and garnish with a few drops of Angostura bitters.

FOREVER SUMMER

NICK KRANZ, THE HYTHE, VAIL, CO

Imagine a tiki drink partying in Vail, and that's what you've got in this Rocky Mountain favorite. The aged rum and amaro provide the dark backbone to the otherwise fruit-forward cocktail, a moodier take on a tropical classic.

SERVES 1

1½ ounces aged rum
½ ounce Fernet, or other amaro
½ ounce apricot liqueur
1 ounce Simple Syrup (page 8)
½ ounce pineapple juice
½ ounce orange juice
½ ounce lime juice
Orange wheel, for garnish

GLASS: rocks

Pour all ingredients, except garnish, into a shaker filled with ice. Give it a good shake and strain into a rocks glass with a single large ice cube. Garnish with orange.

KADO

GABRIEL BRESSANE, BELA VISTA AT ROSEWOOD, SÃO PAULO, BRAZIL

Adding hazelnut liqueur to this take on an espresso martini is a great idea. Adding a scoop of creamy vanilla ice cream to that drink is downright Nobel Prize–worthy. The hardest part of making the Kado, named after Indigenous rituals in Brazil, is having the patience to let the ice cream soften before scooping.

SERVES 1

1½ ounces aged rum
⅔ ounce Frangelico, or other hazelnut liqueur
⅓ ounce coffee liqueur
1 ounce espresso
¼ ounce Simple Syrup (page 8)
2 dashes cocoa bitters
1 scoop vanilla ice cream
Grated nutmeg, for garnish

GLASS: chilled coupe

Add rum, hazelnut liqueur, coffee liqueur, espresso, simple syrup, and cocoa bitters to a shaker filled with ice. Shake vigorously. Place a scoop of vanilla in the chilled coupe glass. Pour through a fine-mesh strainer into the glass and garnish with nutmeg.

BIG HORN SOUR

NICK KRANZ, THE HYTHE, VAIL, CO

Some things, like a whiskey sour with a whisper of pear and bitter amaro, know no season. That might be why the Big Horn Sour is The Hythe's most popular cocktail year-round. Carefully float the port—hold a bar spoon upside down, just above the cocktail, and let the port trickle down—so it sits atop the drink for that first sip.

SERVES 1

2 ounces Buffalo Trace bourbon, or other bourbon
½ ounce St. George Spiced Pear liqueur, or other pear liqueur
½ ounce Amaro Nonino, or other amaro
¾ ounce lemon juice
¾ ounce Turbinado Syrup (page 9)
1 egg white
½ ounce port wine, for float
Grated nutmeg, for garnish

GLASS: rocks

Pour bourbon, pear liqueur, amaro, lemon juice, turbinado syrup, and egg white into a shaker without ice. Shake vigorously for 15 to 20 seconds. Fill a rocks glass with ice and strain drink into it. Carefully pour the port over the back of a spoon onto the top of the drink and garnish with nutmeg.

STRAWBERRY GIN FIZZ

THE COOPER LOUNGE, DENVER, CO

Summer hits differently at elevation. Days start clear and bright, streams bubble with snowmelt, and wild strawberries burst along hiking paths. This frothy gin fizz borrows those berries for a year-round refresher.

SERVES 1

1½ ounces Kyrö Pink Gin, or other gin
1 ounce Fruitful strawberry liqueur, or other strawberry liqueur
1 ounce lemon juice
½ ounce Simple Syrup (page 8)
1 egg white
Club soda
Lemon wheel, for garnish
½ strawberry, for garnish

GLASS: collins

Add gin, strawberry liqueur, lemon juice, simple syrup, and egg white to a shaker without ice. Shake vigorously to add air and fluff the egg white. Add ice and shake 10 to 15 seconds more to chill. Strain into a collins glass, top with club soda, and garnish with lemon and strawberry.

PRINZESSIN ELISABETH

ROSEWOOD SCHLOSS FUSCHL, SALZBURG, AUSTRIA

Definitely royal-worthy, the Prinzessin Elisabeth is a lush, tart, smooth, violet-hued cocktail that's as stunning as the Austrian Alps. You can make your own syrup using wild (chemical-free) violets, or you can kick your feet up like the royalty you are and buy a bottle of the premade stuff.

SERVES 1

1¾ ounces Edelweiss vodka, or other vodka
¾ ounce Chambord, or other raspberry liqueur
⅓ ounce Violet Syrup (page 9)
1¼ ounces fresh lemon juice
1 egg white
3 drops cranberry bitters, or substitute aromatic bitters, for garnish

GLASS: chilled coupe or martini

Add vodka, raspberry liqueur, violet syrup, lemon juice, and egg white to a shaker filled with ice. Shake vigorously and pour through a fine-mesh strainer into a chilled glass. Serve without ice. Garnish by applying bitters drops to the surface of the drink.

SHADOW MOUNTAIN TOTEM

SPUR RESTAURANT & BAR AT TETON MOUNTAIN LODGE & SPA, TETON VILLAGE, WY

Described by the stunningly beautiful Teton Mountain Lodge & Spa as "an homage to the wild," this cocktail gets even wilder with a pinch of activated charcoal. Rugged and complex, one sip of this whiskey-honey-lemon-chili blend will transport you to the Tetons.

SERVES 1

2 ounces Wyoming whiskey, or other whiskey
1 ounce Honey Syrup (page 9)
½ ounce lemon juice
3 dashes smoked chili bitters
Pinch of activated charcoal (optional, but gives it dramatic coloring)
Orange peel, for garnish
Rosemary sprig, for garnish

GLASS: rocks

Add whiskey, honey syrup, lemon juice, smoked chili bitters, and activated charcoal (if using) to a shaker filled with ice. Give it a good shake and strain into a rocks glass filled with a large ice cube. Garnish with orange and rosemary.

TICKLE PICKLE

BILLIE KEITHLEY, BRECKENRIDGE DISTILLERY, CO

It's a good time to be a pickle lover. Preserved cukes are getting a lot of play in the culinary world, so why not in a cocktail? This drink has it all: tart lemon, cool cucumber fizz, botanical gin, and yes, all the delicious quirkiness you'd expect from a pickle juice–based simple syrup.

SERVES 1

1½ ounces Breckenridge gin, or other gin
1 ounce Pickle Juice Syrup (below)
1 ounce lemon juice
Fever Tree cucumber tonic, or other cucumber tonic water
Spicy pickle, for garnish

GLASS: collins

Add gin, pickle juice syrup, and lemon juice to a shaker filled with ice. Shake vigorously and strain into a collins glass filled with pebble ice. Top with cucumber tonic and garnish with spicy pickle.

Pickle Juice Syrup

MAKES ABOUT 2 CUPS

1 cup dill pickle juice (the liquid in a jar of pickles)
1 cup sugar

Add pickle juice and sugar to a medium saucepan. Heat over medium-low heat and bring to a simmer. Stir until sugar is dissolved and let cool to room temperature. Store in a Mason jar airtight container in the refrigerator for up to 2 weeks.

FLATLINER

THE NATIONAL, TELLURIDE, CO

This take on an espresso martini stays fairly true to the classic, only it is smoother and more velvety, thanks to the cold brew liqueur. Built for fire-places, fuzzy sweaters, and a forecast that calls for snow, nothing says après-ski glam like this drink in hand.

SERVES 1

1½ ounces Mr. Black Cold Brew liqueur, or other coffee liqueur
1 ounce Telluride vodka, or other vodka
1 ounce Coole Swan Irish cream liqueur, or other Irish cream liqueur
¼ ounce Grand Marnier, or other orange liqueur
Cinnamon Whipped Cream, for garnish (below)
3 coffee beans, for garnish
Pizzelle cookie, for garnish (optional)

GLASS: chilled rocks

Pour coffee liqueur, vodka, Irish cream liqueur, and orange liqueur into a shaker filled with ice. Shake vigorously and double strain into a chilled rocks glass. Garnish with cinnamon whipped cream, coffee beans, and pizzelle cookie, if using.

Cinnamon Whipped Cream

MAKES ABOUT 2 CUPS WHIPPED CREAM

8 ounces (½ pint) heavy cream
1½ ounces Cinnamon Syrup (page 9)

Whip cream and cinnamon syrup until a very smooth consistency, but before any peaks form. Best if used immediately.

BOULEVARDIER

A-FRAME CLUB, WINTER PARK, CO

Basically the Negroni's freewheeling, whiskey-based cousin, the Boulevardier is a classic for a reason. It's rugged yet elegant, bitter but also sweet, and as timeless as the perfect pair of well-worn blue jeans.

SERVES 1

1 ounce bourbon or rye whiskey
1 ounce Campari, or other bitter Italian aperitivo
1 ounce sweet vermouth
Orange peel, for garnish

GLASS: rocks

Add all ingredients, except garnish, to a mixing glass filled with ice. Stir for 30 seconds to chill, then strain into a rocks glass filled with a large ice cube and garnish with orange.

BLACK MANHATTAN

THE WESTERN HOTEL, OURAY, CO

Think of this drink as a Manhattan that took a detour in the Italian Dolomites and ended up in Colorado's stunning San Juan Mountains town of Ouray. It's bold and herbal—just the Manhattan take you now know you need in your life.

SERVES 1

2 ounces rye whiskey
1 ounce amaro
2 to 4 dashes Angostura bitters
2 cocktail cherries on a pick, for garnish

GLASS: chilled Nick & Nora, martini, or coupe

Add all ingredients, except garnish, to a mixing glass filled with ice. Stir for about 15 seconds to chill, then strain into glass. Garnish with cocktail cherries on a pick.

Boulevardier

FENNEL & ROSEMARY RICKEY

HANNAH HOPKINS, MAMBO ITALIANO, STEAMBOAT SPRINGS, CO

This riff on the gin rickey adds an Italian Alps touch via the fennel liqueur and rosemary syrup. One sip of the tangy-foresty-sparkly blend, and you'll be transported to la vita bella.

SERVES 1

1½ ounces St. George Terroir gin, or other gin
1 ounce Finocchietto liqueur, or other anise liqueur
1 ounce Rosemary Syrup (page 9)
¾ ounce lime juice
¾ ounce lemon juice
Soda water
Rosemary sprig, for garnish

GLASS: collins

Add gin, anise liqueur, rosemary syrup, lime juice, and lemon juice to a collins glass. Fill glass with ice. Place a mixing glass over the top and shake. Top with soda water and garnish with rosemary.

BIG IN JAPAN

ELEVEN REVELSTOKE LODGE, BRITISH COLUMBIA, CANADA

For peak umami, give miso syrup a try in your cocktails. In this BC outpost's modern take, miso syrup gives a slightly savory vibe to this otherwise classic mix of Scotch whiskey and lemon. Sprinkle a few drops of toasted sesame oil on top for added flair.

SERVES 1

2 ounces Chivas Regal, or other blended Scotch whiskey
⅔ ounce lemon juice
½ ounce Miso Syrup (below)
Toasted sesame oil, for garnish

GLASS: Nick & Nora

Add whiskey, lemon juice, and miso syrup to a shaker filled with ice. Give it a good shake and strain into a Nick & Nora glass. Garnish with a couple drops of sesame oil.

Miso Syrup

MAKES 1½ CUPS

½ cup miso
½ cup water
½ cup white sugar
¼ cup honey

Combine the miso, water, sugar, and honey in a medium saucepan over medium heat. Bring to a boil and stir until all ingredients are dissolved. Remove from the heat and allow to steep for 15 minutes. Strain with a mesh strainer into a sterilized jar. Let cool, add the lid, and store in the refrigerator for up to 2 weeks.

THE WINTER'S FRIEND

JASON SORGE, FAIRMONT GRAND DEL MAR, SAN DIEGO, CA

A wintry twist on the old pal—a classic cocktail made with equal parts rye whiskey, dry vermouth, and Campari—this take is just as spirit-forward and bittersweet. Bold on first taste, subtle in the middle, and nuanced on the finish, this is likely to become your year-round BFF.

SERVES 1

1 ounce Michter's rye whiskey, or other rye whiskey
1 ounce Dolin Génépy des Alpes herbal liqueur, or Yellow Chartreuse
1 ounce Bigallet China-China Amer, or other bitter orange amaro
Lime twist, for garnish
Orange twist, for garnish

GLASS: chilled Nick & Nora or wine glass

Add all ingredients, except garnishes, to a mixing glass filled with ice. Stir for 30 seconds to chill, then strain into a chilled Nick & Nora glass. Garnish with lime and orange.

OLD FASHIONED

THE BROWN PALACE HOTEL, DENVER, CO

The secret to maybe the world's best old fashioned? A pinch of sea salt. So simple, yet a game-changer for this classic. Enjoy fireside, slopeside, or even poolside.

SERVES 1

Pinch of sea salt
3 dashes Angostura bitters
4 dashes orange bitters
½ ounce Demerara Syrup (page 9)
1 orange peel, expressed
2 ounces Michter's bourbon, or other bourbon
Orange peel, for garnish

GLASS: rocks

Starting with a pinch of sea salt, add all ingredients, except garnish, directly into a rocks glass. Add a large ice cube and stir for 10 to 15 seconds to chill. Garnish with orange.

JÄGERMEISTER MULE

JOSHUA THOMA, ALPENROSE AND ALMRESI, VAIL, CO

If you're thinking you don't need another take on a mule, think again. By swapping vodka for Jägermeister, you get a whole new flavor profile: one with the anise, cinnamon, and juniper berries of Wolfenbüttel, Germany, the little town perched between two mountain ranges where Jäger originated.

SERVES 1

2 ounces Jägermeister
⅔ ounce lime juice
Ginger beer
Lime wedge, for garnish
Mint, for garnish

GLASS: copper mug

Add Jägermeister and lime juice to a copper mug filled with ice. Stir gently and top with ginger beer. Garnish with lime and mint.

MOUNTAIN COW MULE

JOSHUA THOMA, ALPENROSE AND ALMRESI, VAIL, CO

Think of a regular mule, and then some mountain cranberries show up to get the festivities really going. That's this Mountain Cow Mule—a little tart, a little fizzy, and a whole lot of feisty. Even better that it mixes up in less time than it takes to clean off a snowy windshield.

SERVES 1

2 ounces vodka
1 ounce cranberry juice
⅔ ounce lime juice
Ginger beer
Lime wedge, for garnish
Cinnamon stick, for garnish
Frozen cranberries, for garnish

GLASS: copper mug

Add vodka, cranberry juice, and lime juice to a copper mug filled with ice. Stir gently and top with ginger beer. Garnish with lime, cinnamon stick, and frozen cranberries.

ALPEN NEGRONI

JOSHUA THOMA, ALPENROSE AND ALMRESI, VAIL, CO

The negroni is sweet. The negroni is bitter. The negroni is so deliciously complex that it should star in its own bestselling novel. Sipping it makes us feel like we're glamorous and sophisticated, even if we're wearing sweatpants and have ski hat hair. All of this is to say that this Italian staple is a staple for a reason.

SERVES 1

1 ounce Monkey 47 gin, or other gin
1 ounce Campari, or other bitter Italian aperitivo
1 ounce sweet red vermouth
Orange peel, for garnish

GLASS: rocks

Add gin, Campari, and sweet red vermouth to a mixing glass filled with ice. Give it a good stir and strain into a rocks glass filled with a large ice cube. Garnish with orange.

BLUEBERRY JULEP

KATIE THOMPSON, SPRUCE PEAK, STOWE, VT

Like if a mint julep headed north for the summer, this cocktail takes all the bright, fresh mint—not to mention the caramelly bourbon—and adds juicy, jammy blueberries to the mix.

SERVES 1

3 to 5 mint leaves, plus more for garnish
½ ounce Blueberry Syrup (page 9)
2 ounces WhistlePig PiggyBack bourbon, or other bourbon
½ ounce lemon juice
Blueberries, for garnish

GLASS: rocks

Muddle mint and blueberry syrup in the bottom of a shaker. Add bourbon and lemon juice, shake, and strain into a rocks glass filled with ice. Garnish with mint and blueberries.

SUGAR ON SNOW

KATIE THOMPSON, SPRUCE PEAK, STOWE, VT

Walking that narrow ridgeline between rustic and refined, woodsy rosemary maple syrup and crisp vodka make for a great combo. Served elegantly in a coupe glass, this cocktail is almost like black tie goes backwoods.

SERVES 1

2 ounces Smugglers' Notch Distillery vodka, or other vodka
1 ounce Rosemary Maple Syrup (below)
½ ounce lemon juice
Rosemary sprig, for garnish

GLASS: coupe

Add vodka, rosemary maple syrup, and lemon juice to a shaker filled with ice. Give it a good shake and double strain into a coupe glass. Garnish with rosemary.

Rosemary Maple Syrup

MAKES 1¾ CUPS

1 cup maple syrup
1 cup boiling water
2 rosemary sprigs

In a heatproof container or pot, thin the maple syrup by pouring in boiling water. Stir together and add rosemary. Let steep for 10 minutes. Strain into a Mason jar or another airtight container and store in the refrigerator for up to 2 weeks.

Winter Warmers

"A day in the mountains

ends best with a drink in the hand

and snow on your boots."

—ANONYMOUS

EVERY COUNTRY'S SUN

MACLEOD'S SCOTTISH PUB, SEATTLE, WA

Alright, so your doctor may not have exactly *prescribed this drink, but it's possible that this blend of hot lemon juice and honey (and sure, whiskey and Drambuie, too) just might stave off the flu or soothe a sore throat. Add the curry bitters if you can find them or you can substitute something with warm, woodsy notes.*

SERVES 1

1 ounce Compass Box Artist Blend Scotch whiskey, or other blended Scotch whiskey
½ ounce Drambuie, or other honey-based liqueur
¾ ounce lemon juice
½ ounce Honey Syrup (page 9)
2 ounces hot water (200°F; not quite boiling so as to not vaporize the alcohol)
2 drops curry bitters (optional)
3 dashes Angostura bitters
Orange coin, for garnish

GLASS: 10- to 12-ounce glass teacup or coffee mug

Fill the glass with hot water to pre-warm it, then pour out water. Pour Scotch whiskey, Drambuie, lemon juice, and honey syrup into the warmed glass. Give it a stir and top with hot water. Float the bitters on top, express the orange peel, and garnish with orange.

SHORT SKIRT AND LONG JACKET

SABINE CAFÉ, SEATTLE, WA

So chic and just a little mysterious, this warmer does its namesake proud. The tea-infused brandy and bourbon bring the depth, while the honey and lemon give a sweet-tart balance. Mellowed with a pour of hot water, this drink is total fashion.

SERVES 1

1 ounce Jim Beam Black, or other aged bourbon
¾ ounce Chamomile Tea Infused Apple Brandy (below)
¼ ounce Brucato Chaparral, or Chartreuse
¾ ounce Honey Syrup (page 9)
¾ ounce lemon juice
4 dashes aromatic bitters
2 dashes alpine bitters (optional)
2 ounces hot water (200°F; not quite boiling so as to not vaporize the alcohol)
Rosemary sprig, for garnish

GLASS: 10- to 12-ounce glass teacup or coffee mug

Fill the glass with hot water to pre-warm it, then pour out water. Pour bourbon, chamomile tea infused apple brandy, Brucato Chaparral, honey syrup, lemon juice, and bitters into the warmed glass. Give it a stir and top with hot water. Garnish with rosemary.

Chamomile Tea Infused Apple Brandy

MAKES 1 (700- OR 750-MILLILITER) BOTTLE

1 (700- or 750-milliliter) bottle apple brandy
10 grams (approximately 2 teaspoons) dried chamomile tea

Pour brandy and tea into a clean container and infuse for 1 hour. Strain the tea out with a fine mesh strainer. Store in a Mason jar or another airtight container or bottle.

CHOCO CORAZON

CENTRO MEXICAN KITCHEN, BOULDER, CO

For this velvety elixir, you start with a spicy, cinnamony Mexican hot chocolate, then kick it up with brandy and tequila. Use a good quality dark chocolate for extra richness.

SERVES 1

2 ounces brandy
1 ounce Suerte añejo tequila, or other añejo tequila
8 ounces Spiced Hot Cocoa (below)
Whipped cream, for garnish
Candied ginger, for garnish

GLASS: glass mug

Pour the brandy and tequila into glass mug. Next, pour in the spiced hot cocoa and give it a gentle swirl. Top with whipped cream and candied ginger.

Spiced Hot Cocoa

MAKES 16 OUNCES

1 cup heavy cream
¾ cup + 1 tablespoon water
3 ½ ounces dark chocolate (68%)
1 tablespoon vanilla extract
1 ½ teaspoons ground cinnamon
1 ½ teaspoons Café de Olla (instant Mexican spiced coffee)
½ teaspoon guajillo powder
¼ teaspoon cayenne

In a saucepan over medium-low heat, bring the cream and water to a simmer, stirring occasionally so it doesn't burn. Stir in the dark chocolate, vanilla, and spices until the chocolate is fully melted. Store in an airtight container in the fridge for up to 4 days.

TAVERN TODDY

WEST END TAVERN, BOULDER, CO

The hot toddy has become so iconic that it even has its own holiday. (January 11, because I know you're wondering.) Oh so simple—just bourbon, honey, and lemon—yet oh so delicious, this toddy is exactly what you need to defrost.

SERVES 1

¾ cup boiling water
1½ ounces Buffalo Trace bourbon, or other bourbon
½ ounce lemon juice
1 teaspoon honey
Lemon wheel, for garnish
Cinnamon stick, for garnish

GLASS: glass or glass mug

Pour boiling water into a mug. Add bourbon, lemon juice, and honey, and stir until honey is dissolved. Garnish with lemon and cinnamon stick.

MULLED WINE

VAIL & BEAVER CREEK CHOPHOUSE, CO

Infused with citrus, spice, and everything nice, this mulled wine is a holiday must. Easily scalable up or down, it's a no-brainer to batch up for parties. (And bottle up any extras for great gifts.)

SERVES 10 TO 12

2 bottles malbec or burgundy
4 ounces honey
10 cranberries
10 cloves
5 cinnamon sticks, plus more for garnish
2 star anise pods
7 whole allspice
1 orange, peeled and quartered
Lemon wheel, for garnish

GLASS: glass mug

Combine all ingredients except orange wedges in a large pot over medium heat. Stir well to mix the honey. Once just simmering, squeeze the orange wedges into the wine and drop them into the mixture. Simmer for about 20 minutes more. Cool slightly, strain, and serve hot with lemon garnish.

THE BUTTERFINGER

VAIL & BEAVER CREEK CHOPHOUSE, CO

Use a good quality hot cocoa (maybe Spiced Hot Cocoa on page 69) for this ultimate après-ski treat. Indulge in even more richness from the chocolate liqueur, plus buttery, caramelly notes from the butterscotch schnapps and Butterfinger garnish.

SERVES 1

¾ ounce Bailey's chocolate liqueur, or other chocolate liqueur
¾ ounce butterscotch schnapps
Hot cocoa
Whipped cream, for garnish
Butterfinger candy bar crumbs, for garnish

GLASS: glass mug

Pour chocolate liqueur and butterscotch schnapps into the mug. Pour in hot cocoa until full and gently stir. Top with whipped cream and Butterfinger crumbs.

HOT VIETNAMESE COFFEE

MECHA NOODLE BAR, DENVER, CO

Double up on the buzz with this spiked coffee recipe, which kicks up the Vietnamese java with aged rum. It's best if you have a French press or phin (Vietnamese coffee filter), but regular brewed coffee will work in a pinch. It's strong, it's sweet, and it'll give you the energy to stay up long past that too-early sunset.

SERVES 1

2½ tablespoons sweetened condensed milk
3 tablespoons coarse ground Vietnamese Robusta coffee
1 cup hot water (200°F; not quite boiling so as to not vaporize the alcohol)
1 to 2 ounces Brugal 1888 rum, or other aged rum
Torched cinnamon stick, for garnish

SPECIAL EQUIPMENT: French press or phin

GLASS: glass mug

Add sweetened condensed milk to the mug. Place coffee grounds in your French press or phin filter. Pour a small amount of hot water over the grounds to bloom, about 30 seconds. Slowly add remaining hot water and let it drip through, about 4 to 5 minutes for the phin.

Pour coffee into the prepared mug and stir until combined with sweetened condensed milk. Add rum and give it a gentle stir. Garnish with torched cinnamon stick.

SHISHITO TODDY

THE BLOCK DISTILLING CO., DENVER, CO

Sure, all toddies bring the heat, but this one also brings the fire. This toddy twist spices the classic lemon juice, honey, and spirit—in this case, gin—drink with a blistered shishito syrup. Just how hot will those shishitos be? It's a cozy mystery that can only be solved by taking a sip.

SERVES 1

2 ounces The Block Distilling Co. Winter gin, or other barrel-aged gin
¾ ounce lemon juice
¾ ounce Honey Shishito Syrup (below)
¼ ounce Ginger Syrup (page 9)
Hot water (200°F; not quite boiling so as to not vaporize the alcohol)
Cinnamon stick, for garnish
Shishito pepper, for garnish

GLASS: mug or tea cup

Pour gin, lemon juice, and syrups into a mug. Top with hot water. Garnish with cinnamon stick and shishito pepper.

Honey Shishito Syrup

MAKES ABOUT 1½ CUPS

1 cup water
¾ cup honey
1 cup sliced shishito peppers

Heat water and honey over medium heat, stirring constantly until honey is dissolved. When mixture gets to just below boiling, remove from heat and add shishito peppers. Let steep for 10 minutes, then strain into a Mason jar or other airtight container and refrigerate for up to 2 weeks.

CLAY PIGEONS

TYSON BUHLER, DEATH & CO, DENVER, CO

This funky, Irish-y coffee has a tropical twist thanks to the hint of banana. Rich, herbal, and very perky, this is an after-dinner drink you'll want after every meal.

SERVES 1

3 ounces Middle State coffee, or other coffee
1 ounce Leopold Bros. Maryland Style rye, or other rye
½ ounce Benedictine
¼ ounce Giffard Banane du Bresil, or other banana liqueur
Whipped cream
Grated nutmeg, for garnish

GLASS: Irish coffee mug

Pour coffee, rye, Benedictine, and banana liqueur into a temperature-resistant shaker tin. Stir together and pour into a mug. Top with whipped cream and garnish with nutmeg.

NORWEGIAN TODDY

STEIN ERIKSEN LODGE, PARK CITY, UT

Representing both Nordic tradition and Deer Valley's serene, snow-draped peaks, this toddy is a warm blanket for your taste buds. Aquavit, the quintessential Scandinavian spirit, brings caraway-spiced swagger, while the maraschino liqueur and elderberry syrup add intrigue.

SERVES 1

1½ ounces aquavit
½ ounce Luxardo maraschino liqueur, or other maraschino cherry liqueur
½ ounce lemon juice
¼ ounce Elderberry Syrup (below), or Simple Syrup (page 8)
Hot water (200°F; not quite boiling so as to not vaporize the alcohol)
Lemon slice, for garnish

GLASS: glass mug

Pour aquavit, maraschino cherry liqueur, lemon juice, and elderberry syrup into a mug and mix well. Fill with hot water and garnish with lemon.

Elderberry Syrup

MAKES ABOUT 2½ CUPS

1 cup whole elderberries
3 cups water
1 cup honey, or agave syrup

In a saucepan, combine elderberries and water. Bring to a boil, then reduce heat and simmer for 30 to 45 minutes, until liquid is reduced by about half. Strain through a fine mesh sieve or cheesecloth. While still warm, stir in honey. Store in an airtight container in the refrigerator for up to 2 weeks.

Summit Spritzes

"You can't make everyone happy.

You're not an Aperol spritz."

—ANONYMOUS

BLUEBERRY LIMONCELLO SPRITZ

SAVERINA, KIMPTON CLARET, DENVER, CO

Step one: Pour a few ingredients into a glass (bonus points for choosing prosecco as your sparkling wine). Step two: Close your eyes, take a sip of this oh-so-Italian spritz, and pretend you're in the Dolomites, with chic Italian skiers schussing past you.

SERVES 1

1½ ounces limoncello
½ ounce Aperol, or other bitter orange liqueur
1 ounce Blueberry-Basil Syrup (below)
4 ounces sparkling wine
Lemon wheel, for garnish
Blueberries, for garnish

GLASS: wine

Pour limoncello, Aperol, and blueberry-basil syrup into a wine glass. Give it a stir, add some ice, and top with sparkling wine. Garnish with lemon and blueberries.

Blueberry-Basil Syrup

MAKES ABOUT 2 CUPS

1 cup sugar
¼ cup blueberries
1 cup water
4 basil leaves

Add sugar and blueberries to a medium saucepan. Use a potato masher to break up the berries, releasing their juice. Add water to the pan and bring to a simmer. Add basil leaves and stir sugar until dissolved. Remove pan from heat and let cool to room temperature, then strain into a Mason jar or other airtight container and store in the refrigerator for up to 3 weeks.

CRANBERRY ELDERFLOWER SPRITZ

ELEVEN SCARP RIDGE LODGE, CRESTED BUTTE, CO

Take a flower-filled garden party and toss it into a Frozen*-esque winter wonderland, and you've got this fizzy stunner. The elderflower liqueur provides sweetness while the cranberry and lemon counter with tartness. Prosecco and club soda give it bubbles galore.*

SERVES 1

2 ounces St-Germain, or other elderflower liqueur
1 ounce lemon juice
½ ounce cranberry juice
3 ounces prosecco
1 ounce club soda
½ lemon wheel, for garnish
Rosemary sprig, for garnish

GLASS: wine or glass of choice

Pour elderflower liqueur, lemon juice, and cranberry juice into a wine glass and stir. Add a large scoop of ice then add prosecco and club soda. Gently stir and garnish with lemon and rosemary.

HAIKU SPRITZ

LIBERTY ADAMS, YAMPA VALLEY KITCHEN, STEAMBOAT SPRINGS, CO

This spritz gets it sweetness—and gorgeous bright green hue—from melon liqueur, but it's the lemon vodka and aloe liqueur that stop it from venturing into syrupy-sweet territory. Topped with prosecco and lightly flavored with cardamom, the Haiku Spritz is a super fresh sipper.

SERVES 1

3 ounces prosecco, divided
Cucumber ribbon
¾ ounce Midori melon liqueur, or other melon liqueur
¾ ounce Chareau aloe liqueur, or other aloe liqueur
¾ ounce lemon vodka
¾ ounce lemon juice
1 dash Cardamom Extract (below)
½ lemon wheel, for garnish

GLASS: wine

Pour 2 ounces prosecco into a wine glass. Place cucumber ribbon in a shaker with ice. Add liqueurs, vodka, lemon juice, and cardamom extract to the shaker and give it a good shake. Pour all contents into the wine glass and top with remaining 1 ounce of prosecco. Garnish with lemon.

Cardamom Extract

MAKES ABOUT 3 OUNCES

1 tablespoon cardamom seeds
3 ounces vodka

Mix cardamom into vodka and let sit for 24 hours. Store in a sealed container.

HYTHE SPRITZ

NICK KRANZ, THE HYTHE, VAIL, CO

Herbal, floral, and effervescent, this spritz is like a sun-drenched mountain hike. The rosemary snakes its way through the elderflower and gin for a botanical boost, and it's all made bubbly with a generous pour of prosecco.

SERVES 1

1¼ ounces gin
½ ounce St-Germain, or other elderflower liqueur
¼ ounce crème de violette liqueur
½ ounce Rosemary Syrup (page 9)
½ ounce lemon juice
3 ounces prosecco
Lemon wheel, for garnish
Rosemary sprig, for garnish

GLASS: large red wine

Pour gin, liqueurs, rosemary syrup, and lemon juice into a wine glass and stir. Add a large scoop of ice and add prosecco. Gently stir and garnish with lemon and rosemary.

YUZU WATERFALL

BILLIE KEITHLEY, BRECKENRIDGE DISTILLERY, BRECKENRIDGE, CO

Even though it's related to sun-loving lemons, yuzu, the tart Asian citrus fruit, is often grown in colder mountainous regions. This gin-based spritz blends yuzu juice with basil and sugar for a highly zesty, highly drinkable tipple.

SERVES 1

1½ ounces Breckenridge gin, or other gin
1½ ounces Yuzu-Basil Syrup (below)
¾ ounce lime juice
Topo Chico, or other sparkling mineral water
Kinome leaf, for garnish

GLASS: collins

Pour gin, yuzu-basil syrup, and lime juice into a shaker filled with ice. Give it a good shake and strain into a collins glass filled with pebble ice. Top with sparkling mineral water and garnish with kinome leaf.

Yuzu-Basil Syrup

MAKES ABOUT 1½ CUPS

1 (8-ounce) bottle yuzu juice
1 cup sugar
1 ounce basil leaves

Add yuzu juice, sugar, and basil to a medium saucepan. Over low-medium heat, bring to a simmer. Stir until sugar is dissolved. Remove from heat and muddle the basil. Let cool to room temperature, then strain into a Mason jar or other airtight container and store in the refrigerator for up to 2 weeks.

ALPENBLÜTE

ROSEWOOD SCHLOSS FUSCHL, SALZBURG, AUSTRIA

You'll definitely want to clink glasses and say "Prost" before diving into this cherry and ginger spritz. It's bold, zesty, and sparkly—kind of like the Alps if they were topped with champagne.

SERVES 1

1 ounce Ratafia Rossi, or other cherry liqueur
⅓ ounce ginger liqueur
4 dashes cranberry bitters, or aromatic bitters
3 ounces chilled Bollinger Rosé Champagne, or other champagne
Maraschino cherry, for garnish

GLASS: chilled champagne

Gently pour liqueurs, bitters, and champagne into a chilled champagne glass without ice. Garnish with maraschino cherry.

DIAMOND IN THE ROFF

THE WESTERN HOTEL, OURAY, CO

Once you've mixed up the raspberry-blackberry shrub—a fruity vinegar syrup—this sparkling sip comes together in a jiffy. The cognac grounds the sweet-tart syrup, while the sparkling wine and club soda lighten it all up.

SERVES 1

1 ounce cognac
1 ounce Raspberry-Blackberry Shrub (below)
2 ounces sparkling wine
Club soda
Raspberries and blackberries on a pick, for garnish

GLASS: wine

Pour cognac and raspberry-blackberry shrub into a wine glass. Add small ice cubes then pour in sparkling wine and top with club soda. Gently stir to mix and garnish with raspberries and blackberries on a pick.

Raspberry-Blackberry Shrub

MAKES ABOUT 2 CUPS

1 cup sugar
½ cup water
6 ounces raspberries
6 ounces blackberries
4 ounces white vinegar

Add sugar and water to a medium saucepan. Over medium heat, bring to a simmer and stir until sugar is dissolved. Add raspberries and blackberries, reduce heat, and let simmer for 20 minutes. Muddle the berries into the syrup and then strain into a Mason jar or other large airtight container. Once cool, stir in white vinegar, add a lid, and store in the refrigerator for up to 3 months.

APEROL SPRITZ

LOCAL JONES, DENVER, CO

It's possible that other planets have their own versions of bubbly, bitter-sweet refreshers, but on planet Earth, the most popular spritz has to be the Aperol spritz. And for good reason. Besides its vibrant, oh-so-photogenic orange color, this low-alcohol, balanced sparkler works most any time of day and tastes great in any weather.

SERVES 1

2 ounces Aperol, or other bitter orange liqueur
3 ounces prosecco
1 ounce soda water
Orange wheel, for garnish

GLASS: wine or anything pretty

Fill wine glass with ice. First pour in Aperol, then gently add prosecco. Top with soda water and garnish with orange.

A LEAVE OF ABSINTHE

THE CRUISE ROOM, DENVER, CO

For what could be the classiest spritz of all time, consider A Leave of Absinthe. The lavender bitters perfume the glass, while the absinthe summons herbaceous intensity—and, maybe, the Green Fairy. Pop a cork to lighten it all up in this lingering, celebratory sipper.

SERVES 1

½ ounce absinthe
2 dashes lavender bitters
Champagne, or sparkling wine
Lemon twist, for garnish

GLASS: wine

Fill wine glass with ice. Pour in absinthe and lavender bitters, then fill with champagne and gently stir to combine. Garnish with lemon.

MIDNIGHT SPRITZ

A-FRAME CLUB, WINTER PARK, CO

Frosty on the outside and cozy on the inside, this is a bright, bracing spritz that's made for post-hike (or post-nap; we won't tell) savoring. Heck, you can even say you plucked the blackberries from the vine on your trek. (Again; we won't tell.)

SERVES 1

3 to 4 blackberries, plus extra for garnish
1½ ounces gin
½ ounce lemon juice
2 ounces sparkling wine

GLASS: wine

Muddle blackberries in a shaker tin. Add gin and lemon juice and give it a good shake. Double strain into a wine glass, add small ice cubes, and top with sparkling wine. Garnish with a blackberry.

SUGAR PLUM SPARKLER

OMNI MOUNT WASHINGTON RESORT, BRETTON WOODS, NH

This whimsical elixir brings serious sparkle—literally. A blend of ripe raspberry syrup and pomegranate juice, plus the delicate bloom of elderflower liqueur and bubbly prosecco, this drink is pure winter magic.

SERVES 1

½ ounce St-Germain, or other elderflower liqueur
½ ounce Liber & Co. raspberry gum syrup, or other raspberry syrup
½ ounce pomegranate juice
1 dash edible shimmer or glitter
2 ounces prosecco
Rosemary sprig, for garnish
2 to 3 cranberries, for garnish

GLASS: coupe or martini

Pour elderflower liqueur, raspberry syrup, pomegranate juice, and edible shimmer into a cocktail shaker filled with ice. Shake and strain into a glass filled with fresh ice. Top with prosecco and garnish with rosemary and cranberries.

ALPEN SPRITZER

JOSHUA THOMA, ALPENROSE AND ALMRESI, VAIL, CO

I'm not sure if this Vail-born but Black Forest–influenced sparkler was created to be sipped fireside, but it tastes like that's its natural habitat. A crisp, invigorating blend of Aperol, raspberry liqueur, and vermouth bianco, you'll want to drink it next to gentle flames—even if the sounds of the "flames" come from an app.

SERVES 1

2 ounces Aperol, or other bitter orange liqueur
⅔ ounce Schladerer Himbeergeist, or other clear raspberry liqueur
⅓ ounce vermouth bianco
1 dash orange bitters
Prosecco
Orange wheel or raspberries, for garnish

GLASS: wine

Fill a wine glass with ice. Pour in Aperol, raspberry liqueur, vermouth, and orange bitters and gently stir to combine. Top with prosecco and garnish with orange or raspberries.

SPRUCE SPRITZ

KATIE THOMPSON, SPRUCE PEAK, STOWE, VT

This riff on the Aperol spritz is zesty, hoppy, and 100 percent ready for happy hour. In Stowe, Vermont, they use their namesake Spruce Peak IPA, but an IPA from your neck of the woods works almost as well.

SERVES 1

1 ounce Aperol, or other bitter orange liqueur
1 ounce pamplemousse (grapefruit) liqueur
½ ounce lemon juice
Spruce Peak IPA, or other IPA
Orange wheel, for garnish

GLASS: wine

Fill a wine glass with ice. Pour Aperol, pamplemousse liqueur, and lemon juice into a shaker filled with ice. Give it a good shake and strain into the prepared wine glass. Top with IPA and garnish with orange.

Peak Mocktails

"I like my altitude high and my ABV low."

—ANONYMOUS

ROSEMARY GIMLET

ELEVEN REVELSTOKE LODGE, BRITISH COLUMBIA

Quietly wild, this zero-proof gimlet uses bright lime, botanical N/A gin, and cooling rosemary syrup. Just three ingredients and you'll be channeling mountain air and winding trails.

SERVES 1

2 ounces non-alcoholic gin
⅔ ounce lime juice
⅔ ounce Rosemary Syrup (page 9)
Rosemary sprig, for garnish

GLASS: coupe

Pour non-alcoholic gin, lime juice, and rosemary syrup into a shaker filled with ice. Give it a good shake and strain into a coupe glass. Garnish with rosemary.

FIRESIDE HOT CHOCOLATE

T-ZERO LOUNGE, ST. JULIEN HOTEL, BOULDER, CO

It's pretty much a scientifically proven fact that there's no better way to end a winter day than with a steaming mug of hot chocolate. Heck, this ultra-creamy version with dark and milk chocolates is so good you might want to start your day with it, too. Spike it with bourbon if you want an optional boozy kick.

SERVES 1

6 pieces (3 ounces) Valrhona dark chocolate, or other dark chocolate
3 pieces (1½ ounces) Valrhona milk chocolate, or other milk chocolate
1 cup steamed whole milk
1½ ounces Buffalo Trace bourbon, or other bourbon (optional)
1½ ounces Buffalo Trace bourbon cream, or other bourbon cream (optional)
Mini marshmallows, for garnish
Whipped cream, for garnish

GLASS: large mug

Stir chocolate pieces into steamed milk until chocolate fully melts. Pour into mug and stir in bourbons (if using). Top with mini marshmallows and whipped cream.

ABRAZO DE HORCHATA

CENTRO MEXICAN KITCHEN, BOULDER, CO

Mexican horchata—a creamy beverage made from rice, condensed milk, and cinnamon—becomes even more legendary when served hot. The word abrazo *means "hug" in Spanish, and that's exactly what sipping this drink feels like.*

MAKES 3½ QUARTS

¾ cup uncooked white rice
6 cinnamon sticks
2 cups hot water
1 cup almond milk
4 cups water
7 ounces condensed milk
6 ounces evaporated milk
2 tablespoons granulated sugar
1½ teaspoons vanilla paste
Coconut (or regular) whipped cream, for garnish
Grated nutmeg, for garnish
Torched cinnamon stick, for garnish

SPECIAL EQUIPMENT: blender

GLASS: glass mug

Add rice, cinnamon sticks, hot water, and almond milk to a blender. Blend until mixture is a smooth pulp. Pour the mixture through a fine-mesh strainer into a large container and add water, condensed and evaporated milks, sugar, and vanilla paste. Mix thoroughly. Store in an airtight container in the refrigerator for up to a week.

When ready to serve, heat horchata up in a teapot or saucepan over medium-low heat until warm. Pour into a mug and garnish with whipped cream, nutmeg, and torched cinnamon stick.

RASPBERRY BERET

CORSICA, DENVER, CO

Lapsang souchong tea, which comes from China's Wuyi Mountain region, replicates mezcal's smokiness, and, when combined with the tart acidity of the raspberry shrub and creamy aquafaba, makes for a complex, just-fruity-enough mocktail.

SERVES 1

2 ounces lapsang souchong tea, or other smoky black tea
¾ ounce Pink Peppercorn Syrup (page 9)
¾ ounce aquafaba (liquid from a can of chickpeas)
½ ounce Raspberry Shrub (below)
½ ounce lemon juice

GLASS: fizz, coupe, or collins

Add all ingredients to a shaker filled with ice. Give it a good shake and strain into a glass.

Raspberry Shrub

MAKES 14 TO 16 OUNCES

6 ounces raspberries
1 cup sugar
1 cup apple cider vinegar

Toss raspberries with sugar and refrigerate for 12 to 24 hours. Give it a good stir, push the berries through a strainer, and stir in apple cider vinegar. Store in an airtight container in the fridge for up to 3 months.

APPLE STRUDEL MOCKTAIL

ROSEWOOD SCHLOSS FUSCHL, SALZBURG, AUSTRIA

The oldest written apple strudel (or apfelstrudel*) recipe comes from Austria, so of course we're going to trust the Rosewood Schloss Fuschl for a liquid version of the spiced treat. All the appley, cinnamony goodness of the dessert, without any pesky forks getting in the way.*

SERVES 1

2 ounces apple juice
1 ounce lemon juice
¾ ounce Spiced Syrup (below)
½ teaspoon ground cinnamon
Ginger ale
Apple slice, for garnish
Cinnamon stick, for garnish

GLASS: highball

Fill a highball glass with ice. Pour apple juice, lemon juice, spiced syrup, and cinnamon directly into the glass. Top with ginger ale. Give it a gentle stir and garnish with apple and cinnamon stick.

Spiced Syrup

MAKES ABOUT 2 CUPS

1 cup water
1 cup brown sugar
1 cinnamon stick
2 black peppercorns
1 clove
1 star anise pod
¼ teaspoon vanilla powder

Add all ingredients to a medium saucepan and heat to a boil. Stir until sugar is dissolved, and let simmer for 10 minutes. Allow it to cool and then strain into a Mason jar or another airtight container. Store in the refrigerator for up to 2 weeks.

LET IT
SNOW!

LAVENDER LEMONADE

ODIE B'S, DENVER, CO

We do porch sippers in the Rockies, too, and this lemonade is a standard come summer. Stalks of lavender burst their lilac and purple blooms, like a watercolor painting come alive in the alpine. Infuse some into simple syrup, add some lemon, and you've got this post-hike quencher.

SERVES 1

2 ounces water
¾ ounce Lavender Syrup (page 9)
¾ ounce lemon juice
2 ounces soda water
Lemon wheel, for garnish

GLASS: highball

Add water, lavender syrup, and lemon juice to a shaker and give it a good shake. Pour into a highball glass filled with ice, top with soda water, and garnish with lemon.

BROWN DERBY

BILLIE KEITHLEY, BRECKENRIDGE DISTILLERY, CO

This crisp, rosy drink rivals alpine sunshine for bright warmth. Bonus points for using a mountain wildflower honey for the simple syrup that counters the tart grapefruit.

SERVES 1

2½ ounces Mock One non-alcoholic whiskey, or other non-alcoholic whiskey
1 ounce grapefruit juice
¾ ounce Honey Syrup (page 9)
Grapefruit peel, for garnish

GLASS: coupe

Add non-alcoholic whiskey, grapefruit juice, and honey syrup to a shaker filled with ice. Give it a good shake and strain into a glass. Garnish with grapefruit peel.

N/A Gin & Tonic

N/A GIN & TONIC

BILLIE KEITHLEY, BRECKENRIDGE DISTILLERY, CO

When you don't feel like fussing with simple syrups and juices, the G&T is there for you. This spirit-free version is just as easy and satisfying as its boozy counterpart. Treat yourself to a good non-alcoholic gin for this one, like Breckenridge Distillery's own Mock One.

SERVES 1

2 ounces Mock One non-alcoholic gin, or other non-alcoholic gin
Tonic water
Lime wheel, or any seasonal fruit, for garnish

GLASS: rocks

Fill a rocks glass with ice and pour in non-alcoholic gin. Top with tonic water and give it a stir. Garnish with lime.

CINAPPLE

A-FRAME CLUB, WINTER PARK, CO

You know that last sliver of sunlight over the peaks before the sun sets for the night? That's this drink. A golden blend of pineapple juice, honey syrup, and a sprinkling of cinnamon that's sweet and spiced.

SERVES 1

3 ounces pineapple juice
1 ounce Honey Syrup (page 9)
2 shakes ground cinnamon

GLASS: rocks

Fill a rocks glass with ice. Pour pineapple juice, honey syrup, and cinnamon into a shaker. Give it a good shake and strain into the prepared glass.

ZEPHYR

THE WESTERN HOTEL, OURAY, CO

As cool and crisp as mountain air, this herbaceous sparkler muddles lime, cucumber, basil, and mint with simple syrup. Club soda and a dash of saline bring it all together for a mega refresher.

SERVES 1

1 lime
1½ ounces Simple Syrup (page 8)
4 to 5 thinly sliced cucumber discs (about ⅜-inch), plus more for garnish
2 to 3 basil leaves
Salt, for rim
8 to 10 mint leaves, plus more for garnish
4 to 5 drops Saline Solution (page 10)
1 to 2 ounces club soda

SPECIAL EQUIPMENT: swizzle stick and straw

GLASS: julep or wine

Cut the lime: first, slice off the top and bottom (zest and white pith). Then cut the lime lengthwise into quarters. With a sharp knife, remove the white pith from the center of the lime. Cut those 4 pieces of lime in half crosswise, so you have 8 pith-free pieces.

Muddle the lime (peel side down), simple syrup, cucumber, basil, mint, and saline solution. Rim half of a julep glass with salt and pour in muddled ingredients. Add crushed ice to fill about half the glass and swizzle the drink by rapidly rotating a swizzle stick between your palms, dispersing the basil, mint, and lime, and chilling and diluting the drink. Add more crushed ice and top with club soda. Top with even more crushed ice for a snow cone–like appearance, and garnish with cucumber, mint, and a straw.

MOROCCAN ICED TEA

CELEBRITY CRUISES

Channel Morocco's Atlas Mountains and iconic spice markets with this green tea that bites. The mint and cinnamon syrup deepen the cool green tea base, while the ginger beer pour at the end makes it all sparkle.

SERVES 1

3 ounces green tea
¾ ounce Mint and Cinnamon Syrup (page 9)
½ ounce lemon juice
Ginger beer
Mint sprig, for garnish

GLASS: highball

Fill a highball glass with ice. Pour green tea, mint and cinnamon syrup, and lemon juice into a shaker filled with ice. Give it a good shake and double strain into the prepared glass. Top with ginger beer and garnish with mint.

GOLDEN HOUR

SARAH GOUDIE, WILD FINCH, PAGOSA SPRINGS, CO

It's all about what's fresh at Wild Finch, where the mocktail menu focuses on seasonal shrubs, syrups, and fruit. They use neighbor Sunbird for their shrubs, but the fresher and more local you can find, the tastier your drink.

SERVES 1

1 ounce Sunbird apricot lavender shrub, or your favorite local shrub
½ ounce lemon juice
½ ounce Honey Syrup (page 9)
Soda water
Lime slice or wheel, for garnish
Lavender sprig, for garnish

GLASS: rocks

Pour shrub, lemon juice, and honey syrup into a shaker filled with ice. Give it a good shake and strain into a rocks glass filled with a large ice cube. Top with soda water and garnish with lime and lavender.

Lodge Nibbles

"I have a deeply rooted belief that food should be comforting."

—NIGELLA LAWSON

QUICK PRE-SKI PANCAKES

With a big day on the slopes ahead of you, a muffin just isn't going to cut it. Start your snow day strong with these easy pancakes that come together faster than you can get down a double black diamond. Top your golden stack with maple syrup and sliced bananas or berries.

SERVES 4

1¼ cups milk
3 tablespoons butter, melted
1 egg
1½ cups all-purpose flour
1 tablespoon baking powder
1 tablespoon sugar
½ teaspoon salt
Maple syrup, for topping
Sliced bananas or fresh berries, for topping (optional)

Whisk the milk, butter, and egg in a large bowl, until small bubbles begin to form. Stir in the flour, baking powder, sugar, and salt until just combined.

Heat a lightly oiled griddle over medium-high heat (wait for it to get hot) and then scoop about ⅓ cup of batter onto the griddle. Cook until you see bubbles across the top (about 2 minutes), then flip and cook on the other side, another 1 to 2 minutes.

Top with maple syrup and fruit of your choice, if you'd like.

BAKED BRIE

There may be no better effort-to-deliciousness ratio than this baked brie. The wow factor is high and the prep time is low—not to mention that it requires only three ingredients. Be sure to score the brie before putting it in the oven to make it even easier to dig into.

SERVES 6 TO 8

1 (8- to 10-ounce) round brie cheese
⅓ cup jam (fig, cherry, and apricot are all great)
¼ cup chopped pecans or walnuts
Crusty bread, apple slices, and crackers for dipping

Preheat the oven to 350°F. Score the brie with a serrated knife, making a few shallow cuts in a crisscross pattern across the top rind. Place the brie in a small cast iron skillet (or other oven-safe vessel). Top with jam and chopped nuts.

Bake for about 15 minutes, until the brie is soft and the nuts are golden brown. Serve with crusty bread, apple slices, and crackers.

BACON-WRAPPED DATES

Nails the sweet-salty-fatty trinity? Check. Easy to eat by the fire or one-handed while battling ski boots? Also check. This fancy finger food is simple to make and plays well with a hot toddy, mulled wine, or spritz.

MAKES 16

1 (8-ounce) package pitted dates, about 16 dates
16 smoked almonds
1 pound (8 slices) sliced bacon

Preheat the oven to 400°F. Cut a slit into each date and stuff with an almond. Cut the slices of bacon in half, so you have a total of 16 slices. Wrap each date in a half-slice of bacon. Pierce with a toothpick to hold bacon in place.

Place the dates on a nonstick baking sheet (or on a cookie sheet lined with aluminum foil). Bake for 15 to 20 minutes, until the bacon is crispy.

ROASTED CURRY CAULIFLOWER

When you don't want to drown in cheese, this roasted cauliflower delivers all the warm comfort and snackability. The Himalayan curry powder's turmeric and coriander smell amazing, and your fellow snow bunnies will be fighting you over the charred, crispy bits.

SERVES 4

1 large head cauliflower, cored and broken into small florets
3 to 4 tablespoons olive oil
1 tablespoon Himalayan curry powder, or other curry powder
½ teaspoon salt
¼ teaspoon ground black pepper

Preheat oven to 400°F. Add the cauliflower florets to a large bowl. Toss with the olive oil, curry powder, salt, and pepper so all the florets get some of the spices.

Line a baking sheet with parchment paper or foil. Place the seasoned cauliflower on the baking sheet in an even layer. Bake for about 25 minutes, flipping florets halfway, until golden brown and slightly crispy around the edges.

SOUP

FRENCH ONION SOUP

This cheesy, bubbly bowl of French onion soup has depth to rival the snow you just trudged through. The longer you let the onions caramelize, the sweeter they'll be, so try to plan ahead for this one.

SERVES 6

5 tablespoons butter
4 yellow onions, sliced
6 cups beef broth
⅓ cup dry sherry
1 teaspoon apple cider vinegar
1 teaspoon Worcestershire sauce
1 teaspoon dried thyme
1 bay leaf
Pinch of salt and pepper
Crusty bread, sliced and toasted
2 cups (8 ounces) grated Gruyère cheese

In a large saucepan or stockpot, melt the butter over medium heat. Add the onions and cook until softened and translucent, at least 20 minutes (the longer, the better), stirring occasionally so they don't burn.

Add the beef broth, sherry, apple cider vinegar, Worcestershire sauce, thyme, bay leaf, salt, and pepper. Lower the heat and simmer for 30 minutes. Preheat the broiler and set the oven rack to its top position.

Ladle the soup into oven-safe bowls and top each with a slice of bread and ⅓ cup Gruyère cheese. Set the bowls on a rimmed baking sheet and broil until the cheese is melted, about 2 to 3 minutes.

MUSHROOM SAUCE

You can use the wild morels and oyster mushrooms you foraged this morning, or, if you were too busy sledding, skiing, or sleeping in, you can also use store-bought white buttons. This silky mushroom sauce is best eaten spooned over your favorite cut of steak.

SERVES 2 TO 4

¼ cup (½ stick) butter, divided
1½ cups sliced mushrooms
1 small shallot, thinly sliced
⅓ cup chicken or beef stock
⅓ cup dry white wine
1 teaspoon Worcestershire sauce
1 tablespoon heavy cream
Salt and pepper, to taste

Preheat a large skillet over medium heat. Add 2 tablespoons of butter, mushrooms, and shallot. Sauté until the mushrooms start to brown, stirring occasionally, 6 to 8 minutes.

Add the remaining butter, chicken stock, wine, and Worcestershire sauce to the skillet, scraping up any brown bits stuck to the pan. Reduce heat to low and cook for another 10 to 15 minutes, until the sauce is reduced by half.

Stir in the heavy cream, salt, and pepper, until the sauce is just thick enough to coat the back of a spoon.

PAN-SEARED STEAK

For a perfect, caramelized-on-the-outside, juicy-on-the-inside steak, get your skillet steaming hot before you add the meat. (You want the steak to downright hiss *when you drop it in.) Then it's just a few minutes per side before you enter carnivore nirvana.*

SERVES 2

1 pound New York strip or rib eye steaks
½ teaspoon salt, or more to taste
½ teaspoon black pepper
½ tablespoon vegetable oil, or other high heat oil

Pat room-temperature steaks dry with paper towels and season both sides with salt and pepper. Preheat a cast iron skillet over high heat (you want it hot before you add the steaks). Add oil to pan, then add the steaks.

Without moving the steaks, sear for about 3 minutes, then flip and sear the other side for 3 minutes. (Use a meat thermometer to check for doneness; you want 130–135°F for medium-rare.) Let the steaks rest for 5 minutes before slicing.

CHEESE FONDUE

Make like you're relaxing in the Alps at a Swiss chalet with this bubbly pot of cheesy fondue. I like to mix Gruyère and cheddar for a silky, sharp blend, but really you can use whatever cheese your dairy-loving heart desires. Grab some bread, veggies, and fruit, and skewer out.

SERVES 6

1 cup dry white wine
2 tablespoons all-purpose flour
1 clove garlic, minced
¼ teaspoon nutmeg
Pinch of salt
2 cups (8 ounces) grated Gruyère cheese
2 cups (8 ounces) grated cheddar cheese
Crusty bread, carrots, roasted potatoes, and apples for dipping

In a fondue pot or medium saucepan over medium-low heat, bring the wine to a simmer. Stir in the flour, garlic, nutmeg, and salt. Add the cheeses in thirds, stirring well after each addition so it melts into the wine mixture. Once smooth, serve with bread, carrots, potatoes, and apples for skewering and dipping.

HOT COCOA MUG CAKE

The best winter desserts are quick, easy, and loaded with hot cocoa magic. This mug cake for one is a decadent cheat—all the chocolatey richness of a traditional cake but made in the microwave using hot cocoa mix. Top with mini marshmallows, because of course.

SERVES 1

⅓ cup hot cocoa mix
⅓ cup all-purpose flour
¼ cup milk
2 tablespoons chocolate chips
1 tablespoon vegetable oil
½ teaspoon baking powder
¼ teaspoon vanilla
Small pinch of salt
Mini marshmallows, for topping

Pour all the ingredients, except the mini marshmallows, into a microwave-safe mug and stir together until no clumps remain. Heat in the microwave for about 1 minute. Insert a toothpick, and if it comes out clean, it's done; otherwise, heat again in 20 to 30 second intervals. Top with mini marshmallows.

S'MORES DIP

Sure, you might associate s'mores with summer, but this dip—a true three-ingredient wonder—makes more sense for an indoors, wintry treat. Just layer the chocolate of your choice (I like to use peanut butter cups) and marshmallows, get it all nice and toasty in the oven, and swoop in with graham crackers.

SERVES A CROWD

1 to 2 king-size milk chocolate bars, or peanut butter cups
1 (10-ounce) bag large marshmallows
Graham crackers, for dipping

Preheat the oven to 375°F and grease an oven-safe baking dish. Place the chocolate in a layer on the bottom of the baking dish. Arrange marshmallows on top.

Bake until chocolate is melted and marshmallows are golden, about 8 minutes (or until marshmallows reach your desired level of gooeyness). Allow to cool for 5 minutes or so, and then dig in with graham crackers.

Index

METRIC CONVERSION CHART

Volume Measurements

U.S.	METRIC
1 teaspoon	5 ml
1 tablespoon	15 ml
¼ cup	60 ml
⅓ cup	75 ml
½ cup	125 ml
⅔ cup	150 ml
¾ cup	175 ml
1 cup	250 ml

Weight Measurements

U.S.	METRIC
½ ounce	15 g
1 ounce	30 g
3 ounces	90 g
4 ounces	115 g
8 ounces	225 g
12 ounces	350 g
1 pound	450 g
2¼ pounds	1 kg

Temperature Conversion

FAHRENHEIT	CELSIUS
250	120
300	150
325	160
350	180
375	190
400	200
425	220
450	230

About the Author

Allyson Reedy is a food writer, restaurant critic, and novelist. Her work has been published in a number of newspapers and magazines, including *The Denver Post* and *Bon Appétit*. She is the author of several cookbooks, including *50 Things to Bake Before You Die*, *The Phone Eats First,* and *Beach Cocktails*. She lives in Colorado with her children, husband, and pug.